Storm[illegible] Friends

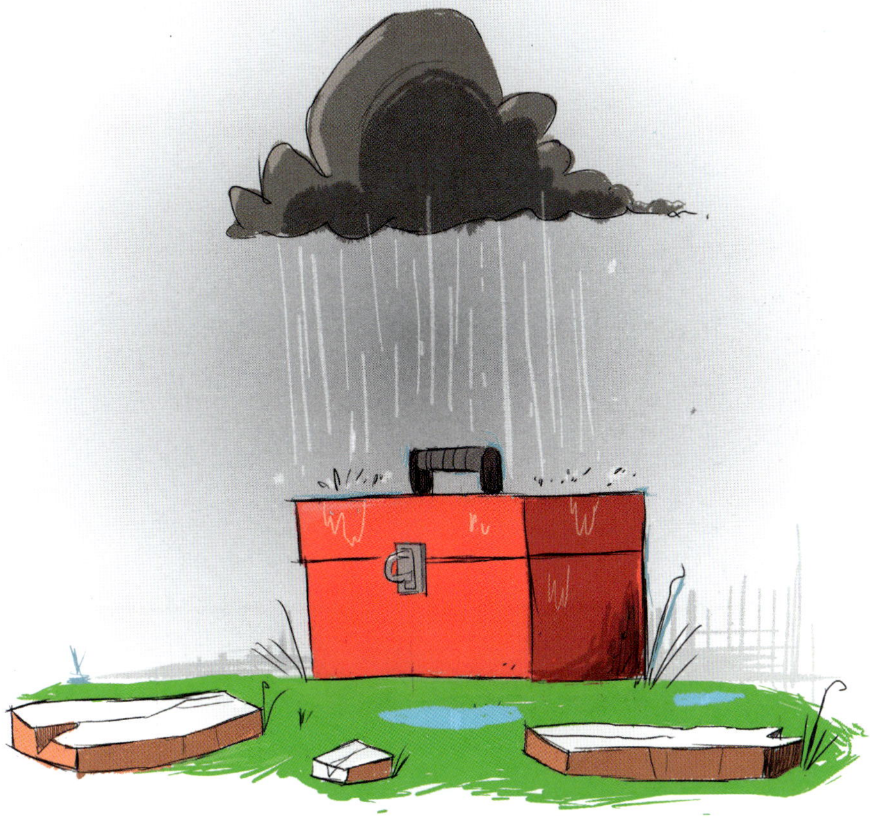

Story by Alison Hawes
Illustrated by Colin Jack

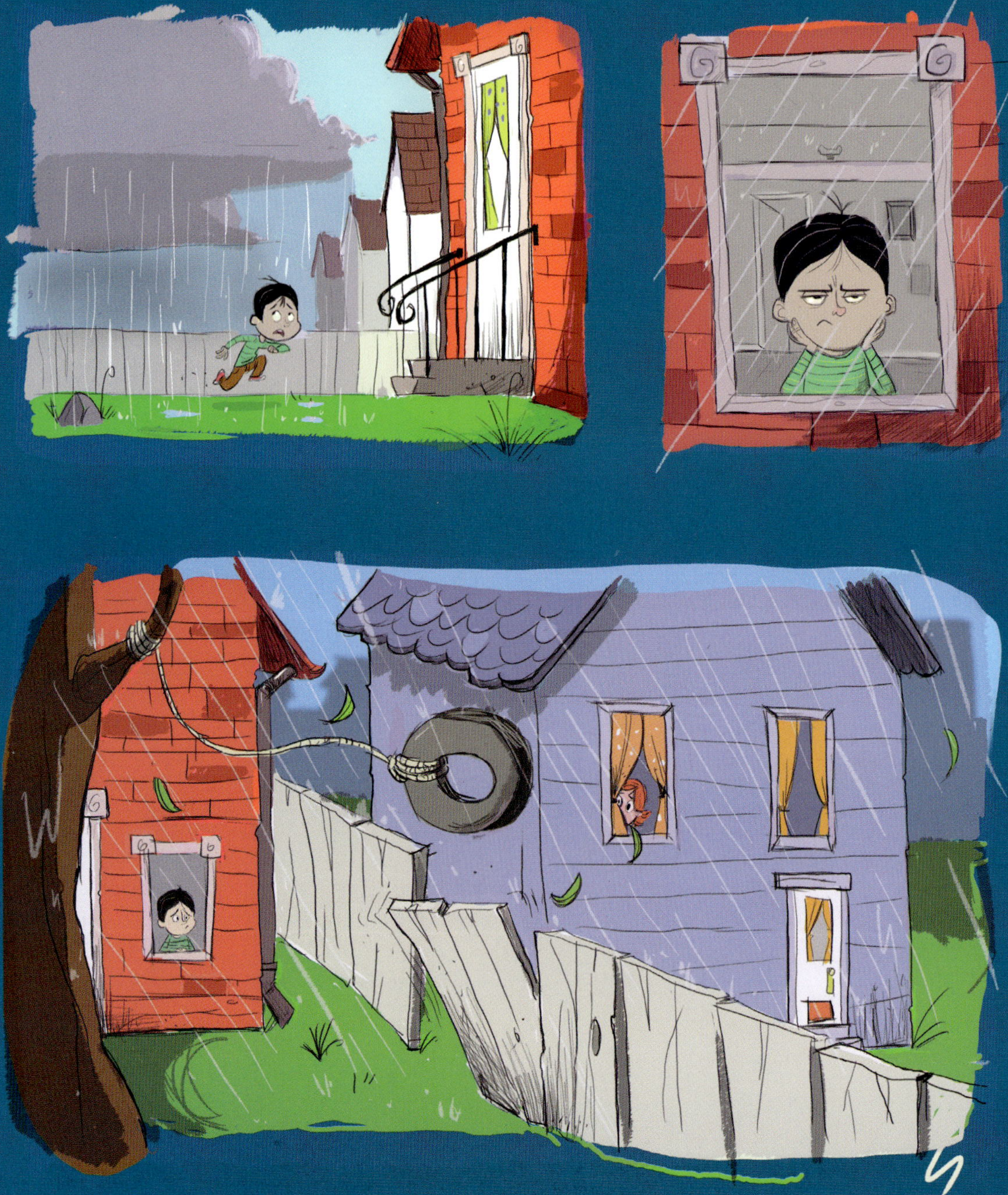

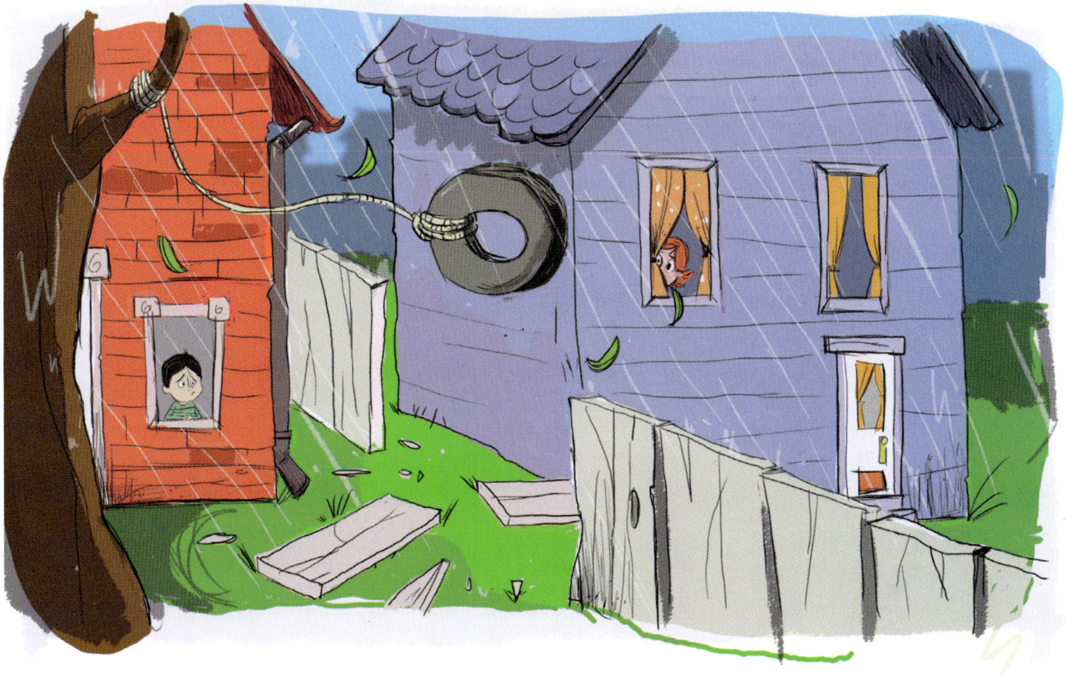

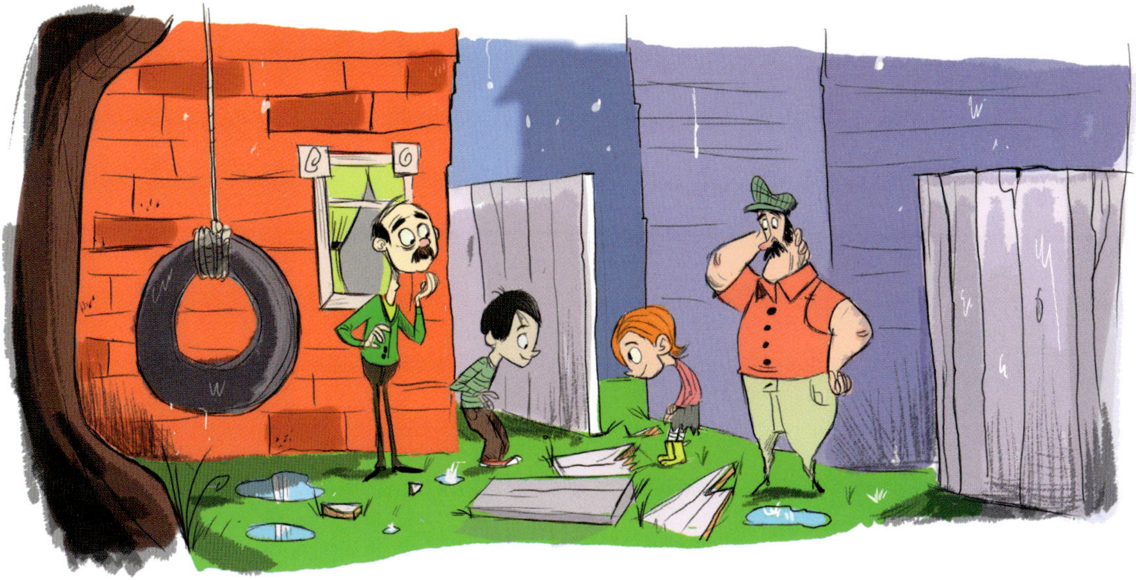

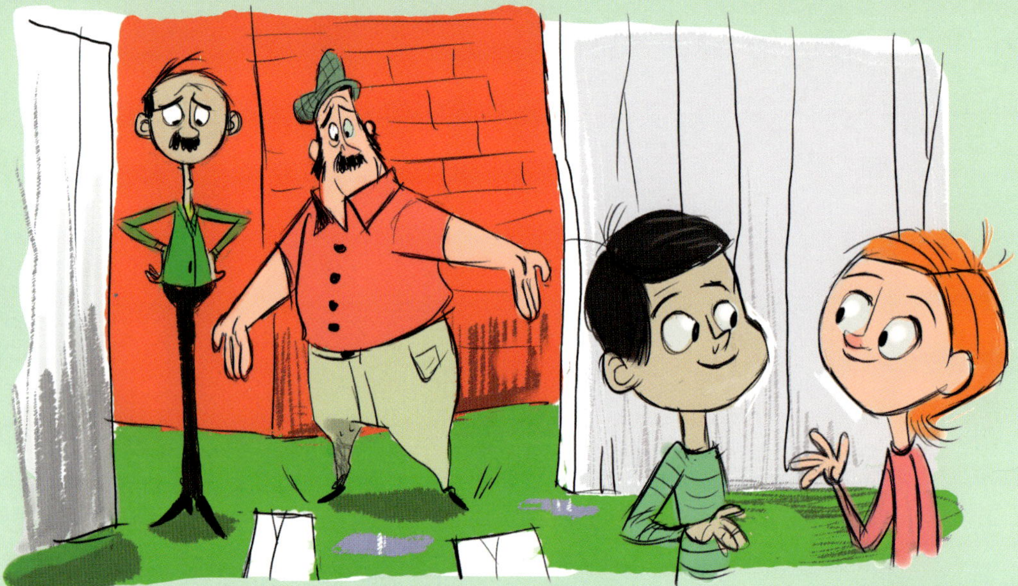

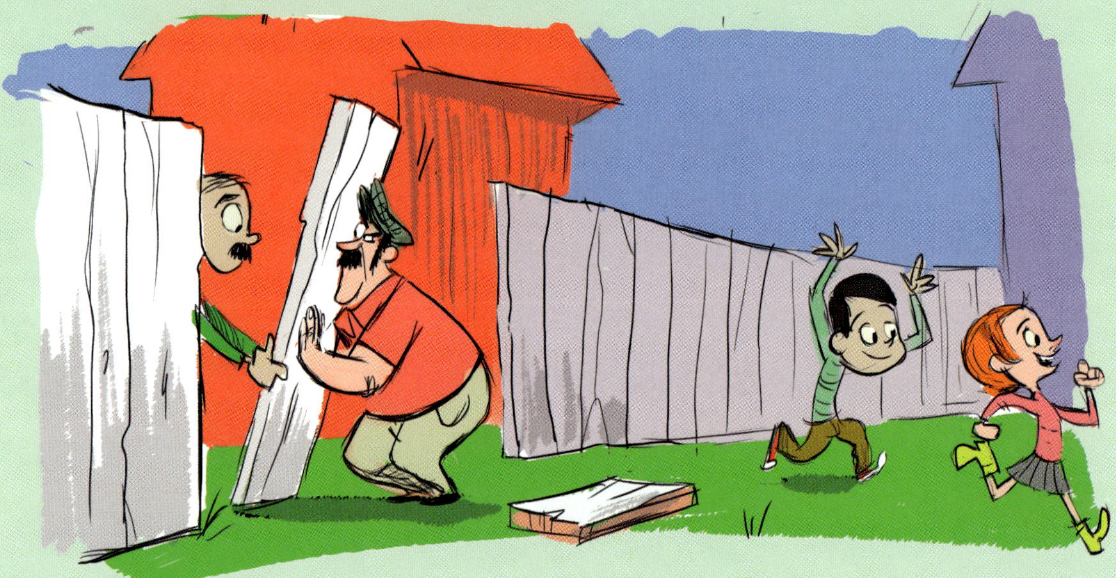

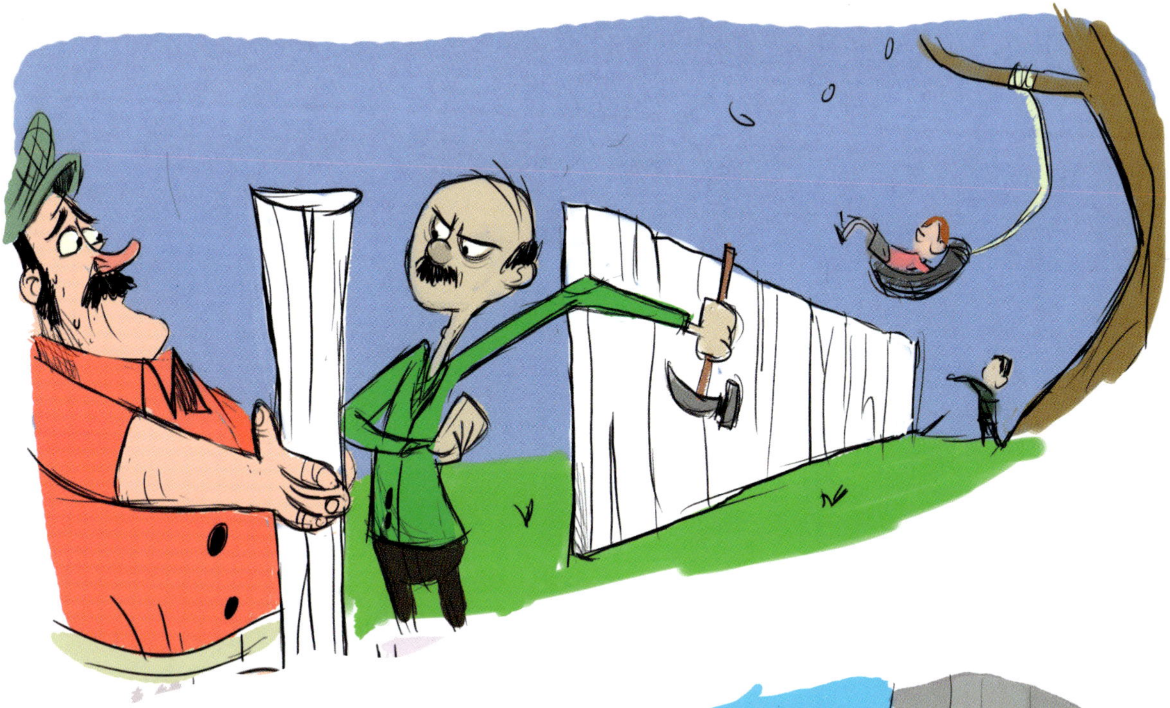

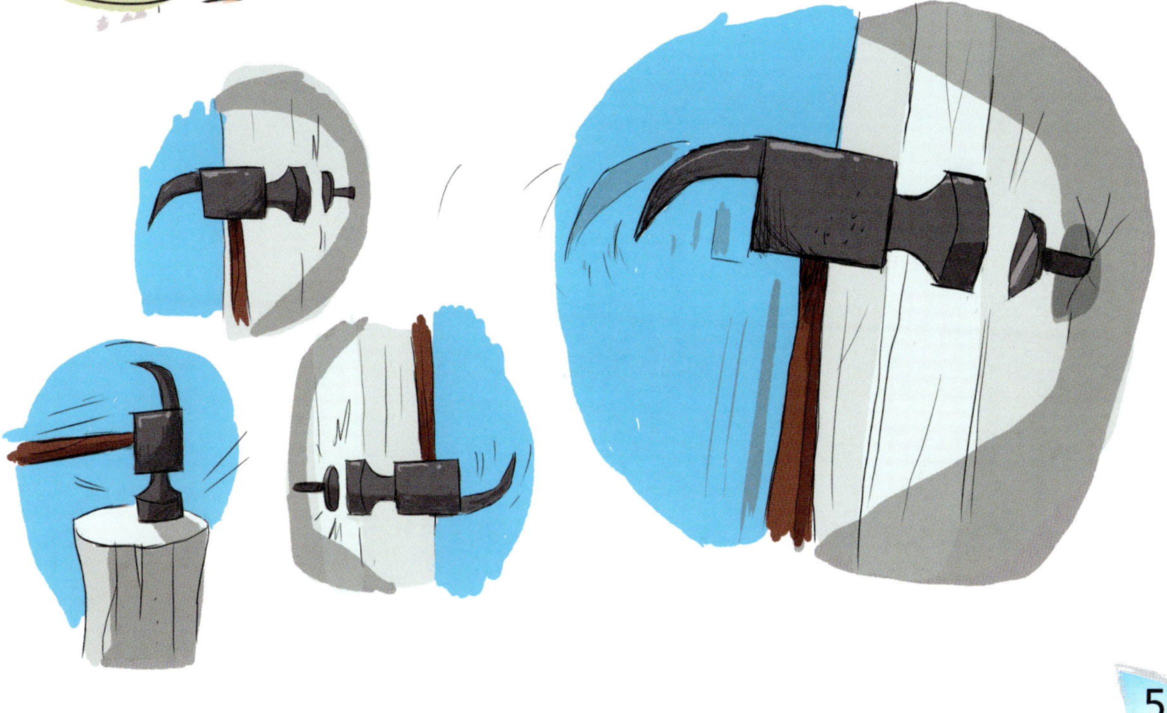

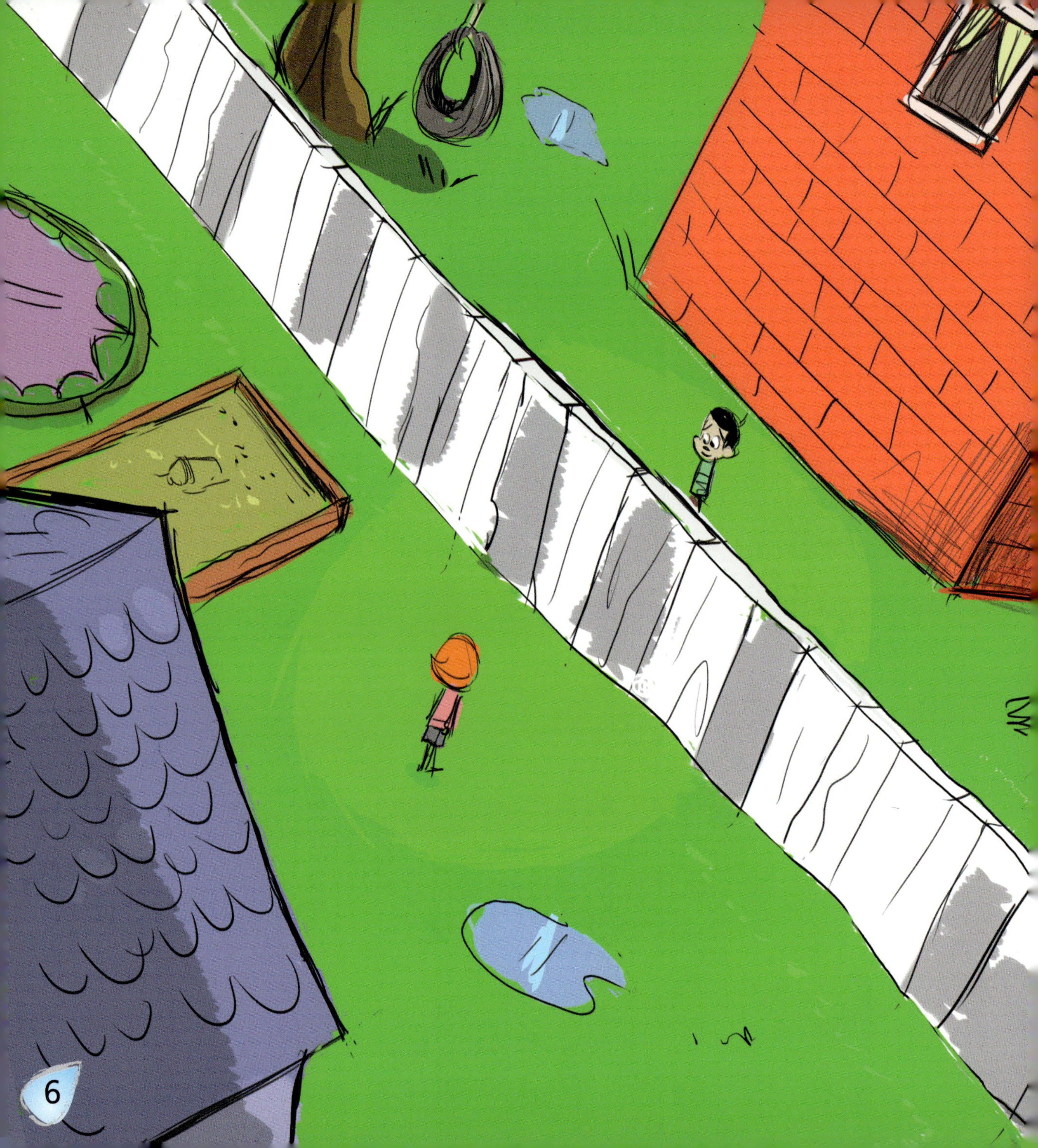

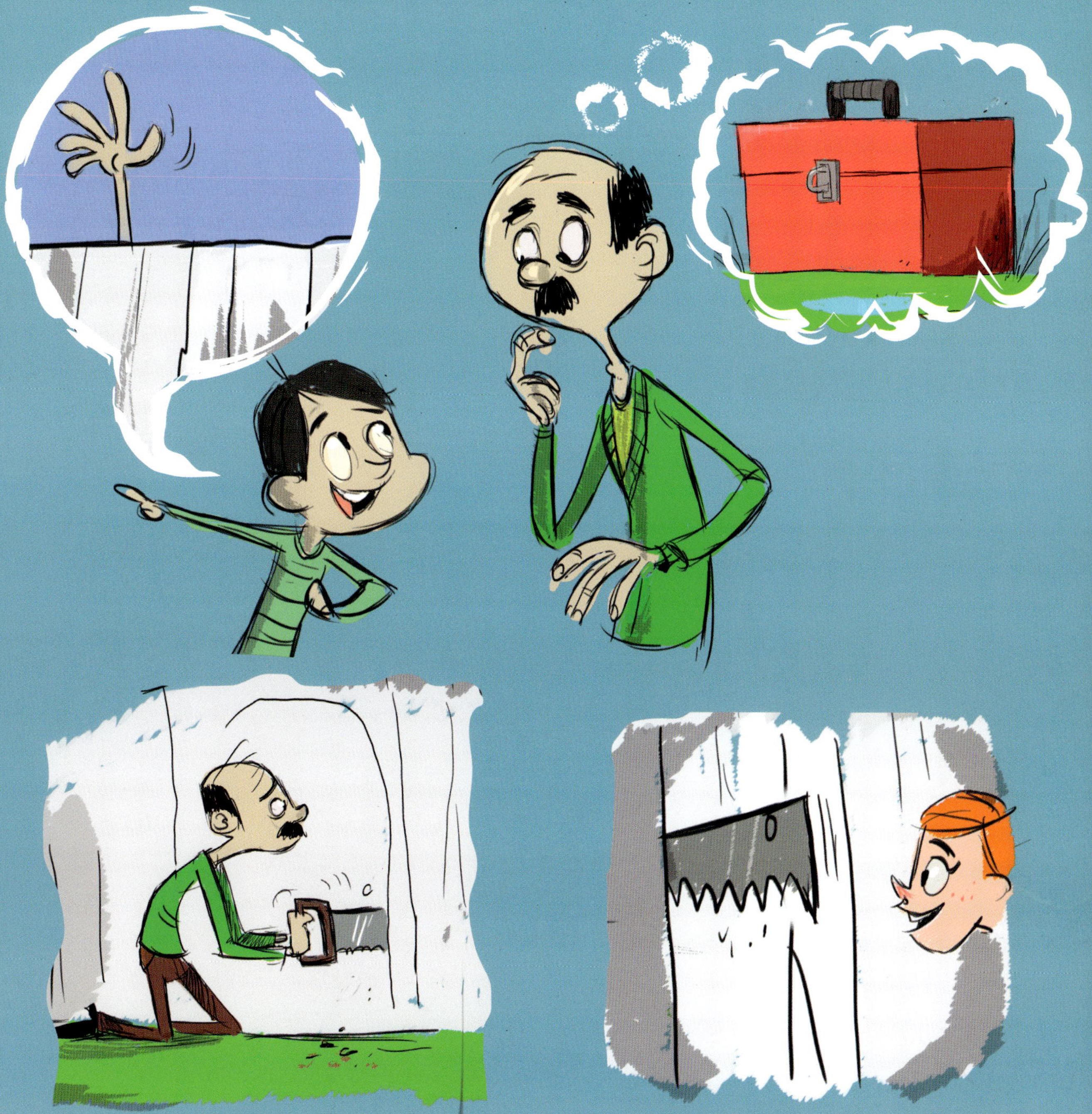

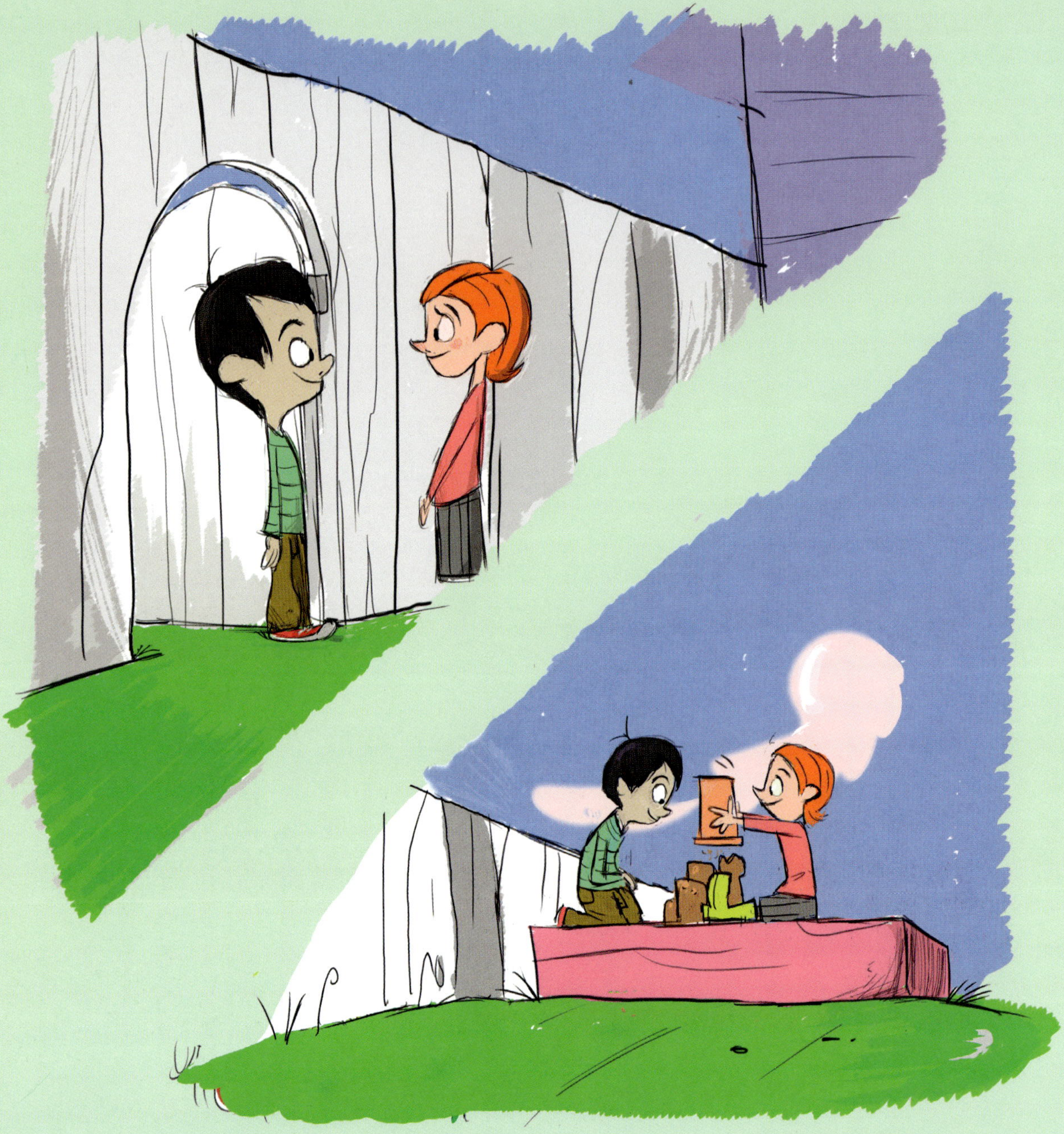